TAXIS

by Mary Winget

Lerner Publications Company • Minneapolis

For Tiernan, Sebastian, and their great-grandpa Mueller

Text copyright © 2007 by Lerner Publications Company

Lerner Publications Company
A division of Lerner Publishing Group
241 First Avenue North
Minneapolis, MN 55401 U.S.A.

Website address: www.lernerbooks.com

Words in **bold type** are explained in a glossary on page 30.

Library of Congress Cataloging-in-Publication Data

Winget, Mary.
    Taxis / by Mary Winget.
       p. cm. — (Pull ahead books)
    Includes index.
    ISBN-13: 978–0–8225–6419–5 (lib. bdg. : alk. paper)
    ISBN-10: 0–8225–6419–X (lib. bdg. : alk. paper)
    1. Taxicabs—Juvenile literature. I. Title.
HE5611.W63 2007
388.4'13214—dc22
                               2006018509

Manufactured in the United States of America
1 2 3 4 5 6 – JR – 12 11 10 09 08 07

Hey! This person needs a ride. What will she do?

Look! Here comes a taxi!

Taxis take people where they want
to go. People riding in taxis are called
passengers.

Taxis wait for passengers at airports and train stations.

Some taxis are vans. They can carry
several passengers.

In big cities, many taxis are on the streets.

Sometimes people **hail** a taxi that is on the street. They step to the curb. Then they raise an arm in the air.

Raising an arm in the air gives a signal to the taxi driver. It lets the driver know that the person wants a ride.

Sometimes people call a taxi company from their home or office. A taxi will come to pick them up.

The call doesn't go to a taxi driver. It goes to a **dispatcher**. The dispatcher gets the person's address.

Then the dispatcher uses a special
two-way radio to call a taxi driver.
The dispatcher gives the driver the
caller's address.

Soon the taxi arrives to pick up the passenger.

The passenger has luggage. The driver puts the luggage into the **trunk**.

The passenger gets in the back seat.
She tells the driver where she wants
to go.

The driver turns on the **meter**. The
meter keeps track of how far the taxi
travels. It also measures how long
the ride takes.

The meter shows the **fare**. The fare is
the amount the passenger will pay.
Short rides cost less than long rides.

The meter is attached to the **dashboard**. So is the two-way radio.

Many controls are also on the
dashboard. The speedometer shows
how fast the taxi is going.

The steering wheel turns the wheels on the taxi. It controls which way the taxi goes.

Most taxis have gas engines. The
engine gives the taxi power to go.

The driver steps on the gas pedal to make the taxi go. The gas pedal is on the right. He steps on the brake pedal to stop the taxi.

The taxi has arrived.

The passenger pays the fare.

The driver unloads the luggage. The passenger goes on her way.

This taxi is empty. It goes off to find its next passenger.

Fun Facts about Taxis

■ The very first taxis were horse-drawn carriages. They were probably first used in London, England, back in 1588.

■ The taximeter, which measures distance and time, was invented in 1891 by German inventor Wilhelm Bruhn.

■ The taxi gets its name from the taximeter.

■ The world's first taxi, called the Daimler Victoria, was built in Germany in 1897.

■ By 1899, almost 100 electric taxis were on the streets of New York City. The taxis were powered by batteries that weighed 800 pounds (363 kilograms).

■ In 1913, taxi rides in New York City cost 50 cents per mile.

Parts of a Taxi

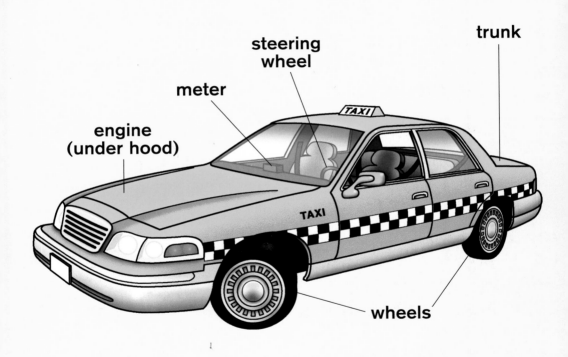

trunk

steering
wheel

meter

engine
(under hood)

TAXI

TAXI

wheels

Glossary

dashboard: a panel at the front of a taxi. It holds the taxi's meter and speedometer.

dispatcher: a person who sends and receives messages

fare: the amount a passenger must pay at the end of a taxi ride

hail: to wave or send a signal

meter: a tool to measure distance and time

trunk: the area at the back of the taxi used to store luggage

two-way radio: a tool that sends and receives messages

More about Taxis

Books

Barracca, Debra, and Sal Barracca. *The Adventures of Taxi Dog.* New York: Puffin Books, 2000.

Best, Cari. *Taxi! Taxi!* Boston: Little, Brown, and Company, 1994.

Jacobs, Paul DuBois, and Jennifer Swender. *My Taxi Ride.* Layton, UT: Gibbs Smith, Publisher, 2006.

Johnson, Stephen T. *My Little Yellow Taxi.* Edina, MN: Red Wagon Books, 2006.

Maestro, Betsy, and Giulio Maestro. *Taxi: A Book of City Words.* New York: Clarion Books, 1990.

Website

Taxi Facts and Figures
http://www.pbs.org/wnet/taxidreams/data/index.html
This website has dozens of interesting facts about New York City taxis.

Index

About the Author

Mary Winget is a writer and editor of children's books. She lives with her dog and cat in Saint Paul, Minnesota.

Photo Acknowledgments

The photographs in this book were used with the permission of: © Todd Strand/Independent Picture Service, front cover, pp. 4, 11, 12, 13, 14, 15, 16, 17, 18, 22, 24, 25, 26; © Ray Laskowitz/SuperStock, p. 3; © Lisette Le Bon/SuperStock, p. 5; © Mark Peterson/CORBIS, p. 6; © James Leynse/CORBIS, p. 7; © age fotostock/SuperStock, p. 8; PhotoDisc Royalty Free by Getty Images, pp. 9, 10; © Jeffrey Zuehlke, pp. 19, 21, 23, 27; © Marta Johnson/Independent Picture Service, p. 20.